Winning People Round to Change
in a week

GRAHAM WILLCOCKS AND STEVE MORRIS

Hodder & Stoughton

A MEMBER OF THE HODDER HEADLINE GROUP

Orders: please contact Bookpoint Ltd, 39 Milton Park, Abingdon, Oxon
OX14 4TD.
Telephone: (44) 01235 400414, Fax: (44) 01235 400454. Lines are open from
9.00–6.00, Monday to Saturday, with a 24 hour message answering service.
Email address: orders@bookpoint.co.uk

British Library Cataloguing in Publication Data
A catalogue record for this title is available from The British Library

ISBN 0 340 772522

First published   2000
Impression number   10 9 8 7 6 5 4 3 2 1
Year   2005 2004 2003 2002 2001 2000

Typeset by Fakenham Photosetting Limited, Fakenham, Norfolk.
Printed in Great Britain for Hodder & Stoughton Educational, a division of
Hodder Headline Plc, 338 Euston Road, London NW1 3BH by Cox & Wyman
Ltd, Reading, Berkshire.

C O N T E N T S

Motivation and change are normally handled as two separate management topics. That is fine, but it misses an important link between the two issues. There is so much common ground between them that it helps to look at them as two sides of the same coin.

Motivation is to do with how people feel about what they do. If they are motivated, they give of their best, and if they are not, they coast along and put in little extra effort.

Change is almost always threatening; very few people like it and most find it damaging to their self-confidence and their morale. So almost by definition, change has a potentially demotivating effect.

Some managers seem to have the knack of making change happen successfully, with minimal trauma and stress. These are the managers who understand what motivates people, and who link this knowledge to their efforts on handling change.

That is what this book is about. By exploring motivation – as a practical work issue and not just as a set of theories – you can be much better prepared to lead a change at work.

This week, we will cover:

Sunday	We're all different
Monday	Snakes and ladders
Tuesday	Some home truths about change
Wednesday	Mapping out the route

Thursday	If it were not for the people ...
Friday	Working on commitment
Saturday	Making the change happen

We're all different

Today, we're going to set the scene for the rest of the week. We'll look at what makes people tick and establish the link between knowledge of that and the need to handle change carefully. But before we go any further, it's worth getting a couple of things clear from the start.

1 You can't generalise when it comes to what motivates people.
2 No one can motivate anyone else.

These two points are at the heart of your efforts to raise morale, maintain positive motivation and keep everything positive, especially in times of change. So we'll look at them in a little more detail before moving on.

Different strokes for different folks

It's an interesting world because we're all different, and one major difference is what motivates us. One person's adrenaline rush is someone else's yawn and what one individual dreads has absolutely no effect on those around them.

Think about the things that get you brimming with enthusiasm, and then consider the things your friends get excited about. There will be several similarities, because we naturally choose friends who share at least some of our interests, with values and beliefs that are compatible with our own.

A simple activity like watching TV helps prove the point. You watch a TV programme with a friend or your partner

and say at the end that it was the most absorbing thing you've seen for years. Sometimes they agree ... but sometimes they look at you as if you've dropped in from another planet. While you were engrossed in a sports broadcast, badger watch or an archaeological dig, they were bored to death. In the other direction, they might be glued to the screen when there's a programme on spiders or snakes, while you're hiding behind the settee absolutely disgusted by something that really distresses you.

So no two people have exactly the same make-up when it comes to what turns them on and off. Friends may be fairly close, but when it comes to people at work there's going to be a bigger gap. You don't always choose the people who work with or for you, and if you do, the selection criteria are (and should be) much more about work performance than personal compatibility.

You can't do it for them

If they hate spiders ... they hate spiders. You can't change that, however hard you try to enthuse them about the joys of the world of arachnids. Football enthrals some people and drives others mad. Your enthusiasm for (or loathing of) the game will never alter how someone else feels.

So you cannot change the factors in someone else's motivational make-up. If you want to influence other people and affect their morale and motivation, the best you can do is learn what makes them tick. When you understand them you are better able to know which buttons to press to help them feel positive ... and which to avoid because they cause a negative reaction.

You do not motivate other people; they are either motivated or they are not. Motivation is something that is determined within the individual, from their own personal values, beliefs and circumstances. Think about a time when you were totally keen to do something and your friends or family were not interested. You cajoled them, explained what a great buzz they would get from doing what you wanted to do, and generally tried to get them enthusiastic. But the best you achieved was a grudging acceptance that if you really wanted to do it, they would go along for the ride, just to keep you quiet. All your attempts to motivate them could not win them round, because no one person can get inside another's heart and mind and change the way they see their own priorities.

At work, the importance of this is that you have to recognise that your enthusiasm is not automatically catching. Just because you like a certain idea it does not follow that everyone else will see it from your perspective. The best you can do is to help them re-examine their priorities, and create the conditions that help them feel positive and motivated; so you certainly affect morale, although you don't actually create it.

Check it out for yourself

Do you know what motivates you? If you do, it can really help you understand what motivates your colleagues, too – as long as you recognise the differences and use them constructively. Knowing how to motivate the people you work with makes you much more able to run a satisfied and successful team. But it's not as easy as it sounds.

You may be the sort of person who is motivated by a rousing 'go-get-'em' address from the boss. If you are, you could be forgiven for thinking that you can repeat the process for your team and they will react like you do. So you herd your team into a room and deliver a speech brimming with excitement and positive messages, designed to fill them with enough foaming enthusiasm to go out and score every goal possible. What can actually happen, though, is that everyone leaves the room feeling stunned and blustered, confused about how to react and put the pep-talk into action.

This kind of comprehensive, blanket approach to motivation can be effective in certain circumstances – if you need to communicate to a large number of people, for instance. But the effect quickly fades, and it's no substitute for getting to know your colleagues and learning what makes them tick and what motivates them. There is no question about it – the kind of things that motivate the people you happen to work with are even more varied and wide-ranging than what gets you and your friends excited.

You can't turn them on ... but you can turn them off

Cast your mind back and you can probably remember working for or with someone who had a negative effect on your motivation or who turned you off. Think about them and the way they behaved; what qualities and personal characteristics did they have (or not have) that made you feel that way?

You could almost certainly tick several of these statements, to describe the person you're thinking of as:

- poor at communicating – you found things out second hand, or too late
- critical, and certainly not given to encouraging you when you did well
- unenthusiastic themselves, although they expected you to produce the goods
- not very approachable, and perhaps not even there a lot of the time
- unwilling to listen, and dismissive of your ideas and suggestions
- wrapped up in themselves and certain that they were always right
- convinced you were wrong when you didn't automatically agree with what they saw as the logical sense of their ideas and plans
- unfriendly and unsympathetic – if you had a problem they didn't want to know, and instead told you to pull yourself together, or just get on with it because there was nothing to discuss

> • unable and/or unwilling to pass responsibility on to you or any of your colleagues
> • cynical, sarcastic and sceptical about new suggestions that weren't their own.

Characteristics like this are not only unmotivating, they can actively destroy your and your colleagues' morale. Even the most naturally enthusiastic person loses motivation and gives up when they constantly run up against apathy and/or hostility

Is this you?
So the first point to bear in mind is that you really need to stop and take stock of whether you display any of these characteristics. Someone else's negative attitude and behaviour destroyed your motivation, and you can guarantee that if you follow suit you'll do the same. And it will be your fault, because you can get it right if you replace all the negatives with positives.

What makes people tick

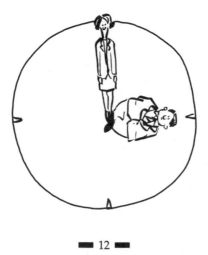

We know everyone is different. Your role is to identify what makes people tick so you can make the right moves to keep their morale up . . .and that takes thought and analysis. We've adopted a three step approach.

Step 1
The person you know best is yourself, so that's the place to start. If you look at what you are motivated by and then compare yourself to what you know about someone else, you are collecting and analysing the important information you need to get it right.

Prioritising your motivation

This is a list of typical motivators that apply to work. Put them in order of priority for yourself – really and honestly. Put a number in each box to show how important it is. Top priority is (1), then (2), and so on down the list.

[ ]   Interesting and challenging work

[ ]   Money

[ ]   Job status or title

[ ]   Appreciation and praise

[ ]   Getting on with your colleagues

[ ]   Responsibility

[ ]   Company benefits (eg car, pension, etc)

[ ]   Holidays or interests outside work

[ ]   Job security

[ ]   Opportunity to be creative

This exercise can be harder than it looks. And it can tell you a bit more about yourself than you knew before, especially about how you operate at work and the sort of goals you aim for.

Step 2
Now you know what motivates you, pick two colleagues at work – one you know really well and get on with, and one who is quite different from you. Do the same exercise for each of them and list what you believe their priorities are. It's going to be a set of assumptions because you can't be certain, but that's OK. You should be able to have a good shot at it if they are people you come into contact with regularly and frequently.

The results will show you that none of you has the same motivational fingerprint, and one of the three may stand out as very different indeed. But what you have is a starting point for knowing which buttons to push to help each of them to be – and stay – motivated.

Step 3
Now get the person you know well to do the exercise for themselves. Explain why, and then compare what you thought about their motivation with what they said about

themselves. You'll learn a lot about what really makes them tick, and the chances are that your guesswork won't be a million miles away from the reality.

Using this technique in practice

It's fine when you know someone really well. But what about the other person you looked at and the others you don't understand so well?

It's obvious that the more you know, the closer the fit will be between the reality and the guesswork; but you will have to fill in some gaps. One way to fill in some gaps is to make assumptions and 'best guesses', where it's reasonable and safe to do so.

Also, try and remember any odd snippets that you've picked up about them, either from talking to them or hearing someone else talk about them. We all come across a lot of information about other people that we discard or store away in the back of our minds because it doesn't seem very relevant or interesting at the time.

We're definitely not saying that you carry out a secret investigation, search personal files or stray into confidential issues. But simply keeping your eyes and ears open – paying attention to anything that you see and hear – helps build up your insight into the people around you. And talking to people you don't normally have a great deal of personal contact with can certainly add to your understanding of what makes them tick.

By getting to know them better you can make an educated guess as to what motivates certain people. So someone with a new home and a growing family – without a salary to match – is more likely to be motivated by a bonus or a potential pay rise than someone who is already comfortably off. Similarly, a young and ambitious new employee may be more driven by the opportunity for promotion than someone close to retirement, or very satisfied with their position.

Tomorrow, we're going to look at these individual motivating factors in more depth, but now that we have established the principle it's time to ask a fundamental question.

What does all this have to do with change?

Motivation and morale are hard enough to maintain at the best of times. But when change is in the air you can multiply the degree of difficulty several times.

Change is going on around us all the time, in one way or another. You will have experienced some kind of change recently, possibly even in the last few hours. The fact is that change, for the most part, is not a series of dramatic lurches that upset apple carts left and right, but a continuous stream of small developments and shifts in position.

On Thursday, we look at why the merest suggestion of change can strike fear into the hearts of many people, resulting in hostility, resistance and even paranoia. Whatever the reasons, you know that change is never easy to manage; your own experience tells you that.

And there's a sort of rule about change, that says that it's the apparently least significant changes which cause the most problems. It's partly because the small changes have a direct impact on your day-to-day life. You can (or expect to be able to) control more of their effects, compared with massive changes to your life that are imposed by the top management of a company, or the government.

Compare a company take-over with a move around the office. With the huge impact of the take-over, people are very worried, but they talk to each other and get on with things while they're waiting for news from above. Performance does suffer while there's uncertainty, but it's all happening out there somewhere. There's nothing the ordinary members of staff can do about it as it's a change that's beyond their control ... so they watch, and wait.

However, ask people to move offices and work alongside a different set of people, or move to an open-plan layout from a closed office set-up and there's uproar. Because it has a direct effect on their lives you get more disruption, upset and in-fighting than you could ever imagine.

Summary

Different people are motivated by their own unique patterns ... what excites you doesn't always excite your next-door neighbour.

Motivation, morale and change are related to each other because it's never more vital to work on motivation and morale than during a time of real or anticipated change. It's always important, but when there's change about, it is critical.

So tomorrow we look a little more closely at motivation and how you can work on it to minimise the damage that can come from unmanaged change.

Snakes and ladders

Yesterday, we saw how different people find some things much more motivating than others. That tells us that each individual is unique, with their own patterns of motivation ... so what else is there to know? Surely, it's just a question of finding out what makes each individual tick, and using that knowledge to ensure they stay motivated?

Ask someone you work with what they did at the weekend or get them to explain why they choose the holidays they do. They'll talk enthusiastically about it, at length. So it's true that talking to people individually will reveal more about their personalities than you knew before, to give you a clearer insight into what motivates them.

And if you asked around it probably wouldn't come as a surprise to find that not everyone is motivated by the prospect of higher pay, bigger bonuses and smarter company cars. The same people who were desperate to earn more last year are not all still so concerned about it any

longer; instead they're motivated by the prospect of more time off to spend with the family, and the opportunity to pursue their interests outside work.

Today, we look at why people's motivation patterns change, because it's important background to your efforts to get them motivated.

Sometimes life changes

If our lives never changed we might hang on to the same patterns of motivation all the way through. But life does change, and so do people.

When the context changes, so does the pattern of motivation. Take someone who's happy with their current salary because it meets their needs. They get their real kicks from fly fishing, DIY, bird-watching or taking part in a sport and they're not motivated by the money because they never really think about it; they have enough.

But what happens if their income dries up, or they need some new equipment for their leisure time? Things look very different now, and money suddenly rises to the top of the priority list.

It works in the opposite direction, too. If you ask for volunteers to do a lot of overtime at work, it's the ones who need the money who are keenest to put in the extra hours. Very few people replace their leisure time with work just because they love working. So when one of the people you count on to volunteer gets a sizeable windfall, extra wages lose their appeal as a motivating factor and they are far less keen to come in and work longer.

The key point is that people's motivation patterns shift, depending on their circumstances at the time.

Success breeds success ...

Human beings are motivated by positive results. As we achieve one set of goals we move on and set new and higher goals, aiming for more satisfying and rewarding experiences all the time. That's why most people start to look more at job satisfaction once they have an adequate income and some job security, instead of just chasing more money. We focus on the things that really matter to us at the time, and they tend to be the ones that are just out of reach, whatever the current situation.

Pat's progress

Pat is unemployed, living in a tiny bedsit and struggling to stay warm and have regular meals. In this situation, Pat's real motivators are the basic physical necessities of life. It's no good talking to a cold, hungry and miserable Pat about spiritual fulfilment, job satisfaction or the joy of working in a close-knit team.

When Pat gets a temporary job the wages pay for extra food and more electricity. Hunger and cold aren't a problem for the moment. That only leaves the problem of accommodation, so all Pat's attention can go into finding somewhere more pleasant to live. When a friend finds Pat a little flat to rent, Pat's motivation is to make the position more secure, and consolidate these temporary improvements into a permanent feature.

Then Pat gets a job with a steady income and it solves the problem of security and certainty. There's money to buy the basics and pay rent on the flat, so Pat isn't driven by the need for security any longer. What motivates Pat now is the need to belong ... to be a valued part of a group, have a circle of friends and find someone who cares.

Those needs are all taken care of when Pat finds a partner, quickly building a good social life and a place in the world. There's no longer a need to find someone to care ... that need is met and social acceptance is now taken for granted. But there's still a gap. It's time to make a mark ... to succeed in something, gain recognition and achieve some status. Pat finds exactly the sort of success that's needed in an Open University degree course.

Pat is really taking control of life and starting to fly. The degree leads to promotion. That brings the chance to work without a direct boss, doing things that really stretch Pat's imagination and initiative. Life's good now; no worries about the physical needs of life or a sense of security or belonging. Pat can make the most of real job satisfaction.

So what?

Pat is like all human beings, where the old motivators fade and new ones take their place as things change. This is important for understanding how people behave at work. If someone was worried about money or job security you may have used that knowledge to raise their motivation level, asking for a greater commitment in return for what really mattered to them. But if their situation has improved it's no use pressing the same buttons again. They've moved on and you have to keep looking and asking, to find out what motivates them now in their current lives. It's a moving target.

Frightened people aren't motivated

If we return to Pat for just a minute, we can see how the snakes take you down as much as the ladders take you up.

Pat plummets

Pat is not motivated by money or the need for security now, with a top job and a rich and fulfilled life. But that all changes when a take-over brings threats of redundancy. Half the managers are going ... but exactly who hasn't been decided yet.

Pat slides straight back down, very fast. The fear of having it all taken away brings Pat right back to the point where security is once again of paramount importance. Before it was about finding security and now it's about hanging on to it, but the impact is the same. Lose the job and the mortgage goes, along with everything else that took so long to build up.

You wouldn't recognise Pat now. The old team spirit disappears overnight and it's every employee for themselves. It's a fight for survival and Pat does everything possible to score points against the people who recently were real friends. They try it too, and there are plots and counter-plots, as individuals attempt to make themselves look good and their colleagues look bad.

Pat is no longer giving everything to the job, looking for better ways to do things and searching for job satisfaction; it's now about survival.

So what?

Just as people move on when they're climbing the motivation ladder, so they move back if they slide down again. If your job's at risk you inevitably shift your focus, from the sophisticated fine points of job satisfaction back to the rough and ready basics of keeping your job.

To prove it, put yourself in Pat's shoes. How would you react in the face of redundancy ... would you carry on unchanged, constructively doing all you could to make the most of a job that you loved? Or would your attention shift dramatically, to the mortgage, the bills and the need to keep your job – even if it meant losing some of the satisfaction?

It's inevitable that you would be frightened, and fear is an immensely powerful force. But motivation is really about moving forward, and any fear that you might slide backwards simply brings out the instincts of self-preservation.

It won't work for long
Fear is the common enemy. It blocks people's motivation and that in turn blocks your efforts to implement change. We'll see on Thursday that the vast majority of people are naturally fearful of any change, whether it's losing their job or moving offices. It may be irrational but the prospect of change always brings fear of the unknown and the threat of losing stability and the known environment. The result is that you won't recognise the people you're working with, as they can turn overnight from a constructive and positive team into a bunch of defensive and nervous individuals.

So it might look as if fear is a good lever for motivation, as it often gives you some sort of hold over people and their performance. But in your search to find the key to your team's motivation, using fear is a very short-sighted approach. It may make a difference for now, but it doesn't work for long. Bullying and hectoring staff so they give in and do what you want, under some sort of threat, is not the effective way forward.

There are several reasons for this, and three important ones
are:

- You are looking for real motivation, where people
  give of their best and aren't limited by the need to
  do just enough to survive the threat.
- People who want do well for their own self-esteem,
  pride and job satisfaction drive themselves forward
  using internal energy, while you guide them; people
  who feel that you're trying to drive them every step
  of the way have no internal energy, so they grind to
  a halt as soon as you stop pushing.
- The pendulum inevitably swings; when things
  improve for them, they lose that fear and you lose
  your hold over them; ultimately they remember how
  they were treated and it rebounds on you.

Motivational snakes and ladders
Keeping people motivated depends on their situation. It's a
balance between:

- helping them climb the ladder, by concentrating on
  adding positive factors that help them climb steadily
  up; and
- removing or reducing the negative forces and
  blockages that either stop them dead in their tracks,
  or start them sliding down the snakes.

You need to do both, not just one or the other. The situation
you're in will alter the balance, but both aspects are
essential. When change is in the air, fear is always around
so it's a major area for concern.

But even when everything is stable and running normally and there is no atmosphere of fear or threat, there are some key areas to look at. There are some very common blockages to motivation that have to be removed before you can take positive steps to get people giving of their best.

Get rid of the blockages

Motivational blockages are issues that stop people getting on to the ladder. They are often everyday issues that lead to a sense of grievance ... a feeling that things are unfair, or not as they should be.

Look at these statements and tick any that apply to you or someone you know, either now or in the past.

- Your boss doesn't give you the right sort of leadership and supervision.
- Your pay doesn't cover the basics of life, even if you budget carefully.
- Your place of work is cramped, stuffy and too hot or cold.
- Your job title doesn't reflect the real status you deserve.
- You don't have a car parking space when others do.
- Your colleagues seem to get better treatment than you do.
- Your company's rules and regulations are too fussy and out of date.

We could go on, but that's enough for now. You probably found things that relate to your life, because most of us do in a list like this.

It would make a real difference if the things you experience were put right – it would raise your morale ... but the important question is whether it would keep your motivation up over a long period. The answer is generally a no.

Blockages

The reason is that these are problems, and a problem is only an issue until it's solved. Removing a blockage like the ones in the list can bring someone's motivational level back to where they ought to be or stop it sinking any further. But giving someone what they're entitled to doesn't make them feel really motivated and committed.

In other words, if you work in comfortable surrounding things are as they should be and you never think about it; you don't have a problem. But if you operate in cramped and cold conditions, it's a problem that turns into a grievance until it's resolved – and that grievance stops you moving forward because the way you're treated becomes a disproportionately major issue. Then someone gives you a new office. All of a sudden, the problem's solved, you forget it and move on.

Not having the problem isn't a bonus or a special perk that comes with an excellent job; it's simply how things ought to be. You have a right to expect to work for a competent boss and it shouldn't be a bonus if you do. A decent workspace just means you can work properly. And so on, right through the list of blockages.

Little things mean a lot
Most blockages look fairly trivial to a manager – but they really matter to the person who is blocked. That makes them real and important.

For instance, it may seem like a trivial point to someone else, but if you don't have a parking space when your colleagues do it can eat away at you and become a major bone of contention. You see it as unfair and unjust, it's on your mind all the time and you keep muttering about it, writing memos about it and chipping away at the boss.

It blocks you from climbing the motivation ladder, because you ask why you should put everything you've got into working for an outfit that treats you like this.

Eventually you get a space. But that only levels things up to where they should be, in your view. It's merely solving an immediate problem and putting right what you see as an injustice. Your success has a short-term impact, but that soon fades and your long-term motivation and performance is not enhanced by the fact you have somewhere to park.

The bottom line is that you have to look at the blockages before starting work on positive motivators, or you're wasting your time.

Raising motivation levels

On Sunday, we looked at a range of motivating factors. For most people, the real motivators are things you'd link to job satisfaction, like praise for a good job, responsibility, the chance of promotion and development, being part of a team, making your own decisions and being respected.

To raise morale and keep it up you need to do more than deal with the blockages. You need to concentrate on giving people the chance to experience the positives. That's more about your behaviour than a quick fix, more about how you treat people than what you give them. It means looking at a shift of responsibility, from you to them, and:

- empowering your people
- delegating more
- helping them plan their development and their career
- trusting them to take more responsibility
- letting your team take more of their own decisions
- communicating more openly and honestly
- giving praise and/or helpful feedback on improvements
- generally avoiding acting like Attila the manager.

Motivation and change

Change – and the threat of change – is generally short on positives. Something as simple as a move around the office is actually quite trivial and it poses no real threat. But if you announce that all your staff are going to change offices, people will dig their heels in and kick and scream – because they're losing something that they now take for granted.

Imagine if one result of the office move was that you lost the parking space you've just been given. The move may save the company thousands and make a real difference to job security, but unless you're very unusual you'll focus on the car park, and resist. It's not an important issue when set against the overall benefits of the change ... except that it's important to you because it threatens something that really matters to you.

It's a hard fact of life that handling any change is not easy. It's hard enough on the personal level, but when you are leading a group of other people through it, it can feel almost impossible. There is more working against you than there is for you, so it's vital that you use what you know about motivation, and bring it to the process of change.

Summary

We've seen today that motivation patterns change depending on circumstances, and that change is not a good breeding ground for positive morale and motivation.

Tomorrow, we look at change and how it happens, and start to think about how to use what we know about people and their motivation, to make the change process as constructive as possible.

Home truths about change

Today, we're going to look at change from a fairly radical perspective and tackle one of the major problems that change brings.

Feel OK about change

The problem is that everyone keeps banging on about how essential it is to make constant changes, and there are more and more experts telling us about the latest techniques for managing change successfully. This builds the expectation that we should be able to do it – everyone else seems to and we seem to be the only one out of step. We do what the experts say but it goes wrong, leaving us with a sense of failure and powerlessness.

Hang on to this lifebelt – it isn't you and it isn't your fault. There are two truths that are rarely or never spoken, but which should allow you to breathe a sigh of relief. They are that:

1   nobody can manage change
2   change is by no means always a good move.

Too many people sit there thinking that they must be a
failure, because they assume everyone else can manage
change, so they ought to be able to. Or they feel guilty and
confused because everyone else is making really positive
noises about some management wheeze, when they think
it's a dreadful idea and a backwards step. It's not easy
being the odd one out ... except that everyone feels like that
at some point. The only difference is that we don't always
admit it to ourselves, let alone our colleagues.

So before we go any further, make sure you feel OK about
it. Don't worry about how difficult change is, and don't feel
bad if you sometimes think it's the wrong move. We're
going to explore those points today and show that:

- there are winners and losers in a change
- a change just reorganises what's already there
- aiming to manage change is an impossible target
- the key factor is that it's about people – not things
- important change often creeps up on you – but you
  can take control
- when you investigate it, sometimes it's better to
  leave things alone.

Change is not always good

Everything you read tends to make change sound
automatically good. Business gurus tell us that
organisations have to constantly reinvent themselves, and if
it isn't new it isn't worthwhile.

That's not always true in the real world, and there is sense in the saying 'If it ain't broke don't fix it'. Obviously, it's right to review what we do, to check we're doing it all as well as we can, and to look for better ways to do things if there's a need for improvement. But change for change's sake wastes time, energy and emotion.

You win some, you lose some

Changing something is not the same as adding something. If you have a problem finding enough people to cover a certain busy time at work, one solution is to bring in more people. This is an unusual solution, though, because it adds something extra; the company is adding extra resources to solve a problem, and committing money to recruit, train and pay new people.

Having the chance to recruit extra staff is a change, but a change like this adds to our lives and makes things easier. So we welcome it rather than worry about it – because we're all winners and there are no losers. When more staff are taken on the new people get a job, the existing employees have less pressure to cover a lunchtime that they don't want to work, and the boss gets a bigger empire.

Most change isn't like that though. It's a rearrangement of what's already there – shifting around the same amount of resources and people to do different, new or extra things. Even if you do get extra money for staff, it comes from another budget somewhere else, so it's only moving the existing resources around. There are some winners – the people who feel they've done well out of the process – but there are also some losers. A manager somewhere had to give up a couple of people from their team so you could have your extra staff; and so the ones left in their team now end up working harder to cover the gaps, doing things they didn't choose, in places they didn't want to do them and at times they wouldn't have asked for.

You can work it out for yourself
Think about a change you went through fairly recently, and work out who did well out of it and who didn't. Then think about who was for the change and who was against it ... and the patterns start to emerge.

So the first point is that any change will upset some people. It's moving around what's already there, and that makes it an emotional lottery with more losers than winners. That is why people resist, and is perhaps the key reason why it's so hard to handle.

You can't manage change

Managing change is like trying to knit fog. They're both vague, they're all around us and you can't pin either of them down. The best you can do is to make the most of change, and turn as many of the negative effects into positives, or at least neutrals.

People are at the heart of change. Anyone can plan the physical elements in a change of offices; it's just a question of playing with the space, sorting out the best places for people and equipment, then writing people's names in where they're going to be. But once the people enter the equation it stops being that simple. That's why motivation and change sit together.

Think about it. How can anyone 'manage' the emotions of a group of people, the minority of whom are delighted at what's going on while the majority don't want it to happen? The answer is, they can't. They can help people come to terms with it, but change is not manageable.

You can cope with change, handle change or work to make a change effective, but you can't control it – and control is an important element within managements, especially when it comes to resources.

That doesn't mean you do nothing. You do have to do the very best you can to minimise resistance, win people round and have a strategy and techniques that will get you to the place you're aiming for. Those who do best at making change work are the ones who try to understand people and work out what makes them tick.

So feel reassured that no one can control the uncontrollable, but don't be lulled into a false sense of security. You still have to work at it, hard.

Change happens around you

There are two sorts of change that happen to you and around you, without you planning it. There's gradual change, and sudden upheaval. You may not be able to control people's feelings, but you can take some control here.

A car's performance can change suddenly or gradually. A sudden breakdown is immediately obvious and we have to do something about it. But a gradual change is an imperceptible decline in fuel consumption, losing a tenth of a mile per gallon every couple of months. The gradual decline goes unnoticed for ages, often until it's too late. There's a real problem but we simply don't notice. Things change so slightly over time that we constantly adjust our expectations, so that what we see becomes normal.

Gradual changes are quite often the most important and this is where we can take some control and link them to continuous improvement, and issues like customer service, quality and operational efficiency.

Nip it in the bud

You know someone who's been on a diet. We all do. They know how they're doing because they weigh themselves to check progress. They decide to diet so they weigh themselves before they start, and again at regular intervals. They plan a gradual change and use a measuring process to take control.

We need a control process for all gradual change, to spot what's happening and take relevant action. Often the trigger for the process is no more than an itchy feeling that something isn't quite like it was. For the dieter it is something like a pair of trousers feeling tighter than they were, and for the driver it's a growing feeling that they're putting more fuel in the car than they used to.

As soon as there's the slightest feeling that something is changing and you're not sure how or why, take control with a technique like this one. Take these five steps:

1 *Clarify the standard* – how many miles a gallon, how long to reply to a letter, or how many hours overtime should this take?
2 *Measure the reality* – find out what the present situation is and quantify it as far as possible.
3 *Investigate the cause of any discrepancy* – and don't jump to conclusions; just because it was a small fuel leak last time, it doesn't mean it is again.
4 *Identify the actual cause* – pin it down and make it really specific.
5 *Find ways of overcoming the problem* – so you get back to the standard – and implement them.

For instance, if you're getting a lot of letters complaining that you haven't replied to an earlier letter sent, warning bells should start to ring. You don't know exactly what is happening, but you do know that all the managers get their typing done by the same pool of people. So, to find out what's happening and what you can do about it, you implement the five steps.

1 It should take no more than three days to answer a letter; that's the policy.
2 Some managers get their letters out in under two days, but the average is five, sometimes a lot more – and you know because you checked the dates on letters that came in, and the replies that went out.

3 You get together all the people who have a stake in the problem – including the people who type the letters. You simply state the situation and they talk it through with you.

4 You discover that the computer keeps going down, and that since some experienced typists left you've had a succession of new staff.

5 You talk to the IT team and find they can sort out the computer, so that's a large chunk of the problem solved at a stroke.

   The new staff issue is more problematic, but the real reason is that some managers are leaning on them to do all their work first – so some letters are going out immediately, while others wait for days.

   The answer here is to straighten out the managers who are trying to jump the queue, and make it clear to the typists that they come to you, if they feel under any undue pressure.

The result is that letters flow properly again ... because of the five steps.

With these five steps you can uncover small, simple and often painless changes that add real value and make a real difference. There's a maxim in quality management that says you can only improve what you can measure. In other words, you can only take control if you analyse what's happening and find out where you can do better, with a planned process to stop changes slipping by unnoticed.

The costs and benefits

Not all change is automatically for the better. If there are more potential losers than winners you have to ask whether it's worth it – especially if the losers include customers or clients.

Before you launch into any change programme, ask the critical question.

Will the result give us enough gain to make it worth doing?

If the answer is that the gains heavily outweigh the costs – fine. Go ahead. But if not, or if it's marginal and you will lose almost as much as you gain, slow right down and consider whether to bale out now.

Check it out
The benefits are on one side of the equation, the costs on the other. And the costs aren't just money. They are disruption, a potential drop in morale, the time someone has to spend driving a change through, and a whole range of other issues, from training for new skills to reprinting letterheads.

It's simply a question of listing all the benefits down one side of a piece of paper, and all the costs down the other. Where the balance falls is where you make your decisions, either to change or to stay as you are. Be honest and fair as you evaluate all the factors, on each side. You're bound to have an in-built bias towards one side or the other, and you must put that away.

Whenever possible, brainstorm the issues with other people to broaden the view – and then evaluate the pros and cons in a larger group as well, to balance out any prejudices and preferences.

Even when several of you work at it, it isn't a neat equation. Not everything has the same weight and one or two factors will make a huge difference, while others are fairly minor. Quite often there's a critical factor, that almost makes the decision for you. When you find one of these, don't try and rationalise it away and say it will be alright, because it won't. So if you know the union will strike if you try and implement a new process, don't kid yourself or anyone else that they'll come round in the end. Or if you need £40,000 for an IT improvement and there's £13,000 available, don't shut your eyes and hope something will turn up. It won't.

In both cases, it's odds on that you would achieve something; but it will mean stress, disruption, division and a massive drop in morale and output.

So:

- involve other people who can make a contribution
- make sure you avoid any bias, so your results are honest and neutral
- list all the pros and cons – including the emotional ones
- look for 'heavy' factors, and especially critical factors
- don't try to bend reality; it may be hard to accept but facts are facts.

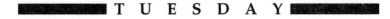

Summary

Today, we've looked at some myths around change, and tried to make it feel OK to be uncertain and concerned about managing it. You still have to work at it, but you can use what you know about people and their motivation.

There are techniques that can be used, for reviewing what's changing around you, and deciding whether a change is worth making, once you've looked at the costs and benefits.

We've also said that you need a strategy for change, even though it's not completely controllable, so tomorrow we'll look at the strategic issues in detail, so you can build a plan for change.

Mapping out the route

Yesterday, we looked at how difficult it is to handle change, and one of the key points is that you have to be certain that making the change is going to be worth all the effort, disruption and time.

If it is, then it's time for a change. But don't forget that even when the list of advantages outweighs the list of disadvantages, there's still a negative side of the equation. The issues you listed as problems and disadvantages now become a reality and need handling as you work to plan the change.

Ignoring the problems and jumping blindly into action is completely the wrong move. You have to plan and think the whole process through, very carefully, which is why today we're looking at what goes into a strategy for change, and how it helps you achieve positive results.

Exceptions to the rules

Most change strategies involve an element of communicating the details, in order to win people round. But in some situations the only option is to keep the plans secret and launch the change on an unsuspecting world. This approach is not often talked about, because it:

- feels authoritarian and devious
- is out of step with the modern line of management thinking that centres on involvement, participation and communication.

But there are times when it is essential. There is no advantage in sharing with the workforce the details of a commercially confidential or sensitive change. Only those at the very top of the organisation have any influence over a potential take-over by another company, the need to restructure to avoid insolvency, or plans to open a new branch, for instance.

So, while the skeleton of our strategy for change does apply to these top management and board level business issues, in this book we are concentrating on the majority of change, that comes day to day and is the province of managers nearer the middle of an organisation. All we ask is that you recognise that the option to impose a change does exist ... because it has to.

Locking and unlocking

You can see change as a process where you:

- start with something static and locked in place (the way things are now)

- unlock it, so you can move it (and while it's not fixed, make the changes)
- then lock it in place again (once you've changed what you want to change).

If you think of the status quo as a ball on the table, you can imagine that there are forces on opposite sides, like hands pushing at it to try and move it. The forces in one direction are trying to make a change and the forces in the opposite direction are trying to push things back so they don't progress. All the time the forces are equal the ball stays still and nothing changes.

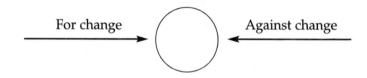

For change → ⟲ ← Against change

It's only when one of the forces gets stronger than the other that the ball shifts.

So what?
If you are trying to make a change happen, you can only succeed if you make the forces unstable, move the ball and then stabilise the forces again. It will not be a success unless you do something to reduce the forces working against you and strengthen the forces that are on your side.

You need a strategy – but not one that's based on the practical details of the change. So, if the change is an office move, your strategy does not cover booking the removal van, labelling all the desks and working out who sits where. That's basic organisation. A change strategy is based on altering the balance between the forces, because these are the sources of energy that either drive or hold back the change. To strengthen the forces that are helping you and reduce the ones that will hold you back, you have to work out what these forces are, how strong they are and how to alter them.

A checklist for an effective change strategy

These are the main stages in the strategy.

1 Work out what you want to change and why. If the benefits don't outweigh the costs by a wide enough margin, don't do it. Don't make changes for the sake of it.
2 Get a picture of what the world will look like once it's all over. Work out the specific advantages and differences, and imagine it all working smoothly. Think about the problem areas as well.
3 Identify all the factors on your side. List everything that is working for you (eg top management support, government legislation, some staff keen on improvement, a new set of premises, etc).
4 List everything that is against you (could be union reluctance, a vacancy in a key post, some staff against it, not much budget, etc).
5 You won't be able to tackle every single issue, so work out which are the key factors on each side – which ones will have the greatest impact for the least effort.
6 Draw up a plan for each of the key factors – to

---

weaken the resistance of each of the key negatives, and strengthen the key positives.

7 Before you take action, just have a final check to ensure that your plans will achieve what you want them to.

8 Implement the plans and monitor what happens, making adjustments as you go.

We'll now look at each one in turn – starting with number two, because we covered the need to check that the change is worthwhile, yesterday.

What the world will look like when it's all over

Before making any detailed plans, get the big picture. Think ahead to the time when the upheaval of making the change is just a memory, and everything is now running smoothly, with all the changes in place. Imagine it all happening, just as if you were watching a video of the world then, after it is all over.

The reason for doing this is that it helps to have a long-term vision, which:

- maintains your faith in what you're doing, even when things get tough
- gives you a picture to share with the people you are leading through the change
- makes it easier to explain the overall benefits in a way that others can see
- acts as a benchmark when you are checking your strategy (number seven in the checklist)
- gives you the chance to spot any possible glitches, that might arise as a result of the changes.

The force is with you

Now make a list of all the factors and forces that are going to be helpful to you as you work at implementing the change. For instance, imagine you are going to move your section, and all its work, from an annexe into a part of the main building that's been used by another group, who do the back-up administration for your section. You might find these factors – which are in no particular order and not comprehensive – are among the helpful ones.

- You have top-level support, as the Chief Executive has said it's an excellent idea – as long as you can make it work.
- Your staff have been saying for months that this change was needed, so you have a good measure of front-line support as well.
- The financial costs of the change are covered from a central budget, so you don't have to trim back anything from your own work area.

- The change will give the staff the tearoom they've always wanted.
- The change just happens to cover some other areas you would need to look at anyway (eg a health and safety regulation that's coming in next year, that you can now deal with in advance).
- Your team is fairly progressive and creative; they generally trust and listen to you, so you're sure of a fair hearing and a measure of automatic support.
- You will be able to produce more, and market research shows that the change will mean more job security for your people.

Forces of darkness

Now you know what sort of support you have, from people and from other factors, it's important to look at the other side of the equation and list all the factors that will block or hinder your efforts to change.

Some examples are:

- You have no real support from your immediate line manager.
- There is antagonism from the group of people you are displacing.
- Their union representative is forceful and will put up strong resistance.
- Everyone has memories of an earlier attempt to do something similar, that failed.
- The budget is not quite enough to make the changes in full, or at the right quality.

- Some of your own people will have to travel further to work, and will resist the move either passively or actively.
- Your deputy left recently and you haven't appointed a replacement, so you will be stretched implementing the change and keeping day-to-day work running.
- You need to stop production for 24 hours, while the change is made.
- You have a few members of staff that you know just hate change, in any form.

Critical factors

You first have to ask whether there are any critical factors on either side of your list. Are any of the positive forces so strong that they leave you no option but to push ahead, or are any of the negatives powerful enough to stop the whole thing dead?

On the positive side, there's one fairly overwhelming factor; the Chief Executive (CE) likes the idea, and although it's left to you to make the final decision, you know that it would look bad if you couldn't see it through.

On the negative side, you might decide that the money is a critical issue. There isn't enough to do the whole job, and if you launch in without looking ahead you could find you're 90% of the way through, but then can't fund the vital last stage. That scenario is bound to end up as a failure.

In that case, you only have three options.

1 Abandon the whole idea.
2 Get more money from somewhere (for certain, before you start).
3 Amend the scale and scope of the changes you plan to make, if it's possible.

For now, let's assume that you are not prepared to take option one. You try option two, going to the CE because you know that there is support in that quarter; you get a lot of sympathy and no extra cash. Option three is possible and it's the only way to go, now.

You redesign the shape of the change, keeping the priority elements (that include the new tearoom, as it would be dangerous to chop out a major plus factor). You lose some of the less essential areas that would have been a bonus, but are not absolutely crucial.

This may feel like a disappointment, but actually it's a huge success. Pause for a minute and you'll see that you have dealt with a major negative force (lack of money) once and for all, by changing the shape of the change so you can fund it. Money is no longer on your list of negative forces.

Pick the key factors

Not every factor will be as important as the others. Some

will be fairly insignificant, while others might be quite critical, and the secret is to select the factors that have the greatest impact on the change (for good or bad) and then narrow it down to the ones which you can influence with the least amount of effort or trouble.

You've dealt with the financial question so you decide your key factors are:

For you	Against you
Support from the CE	Lack of support from your line manager
Increased job security	Antagonism from the other section
Good support from a loyal team	Some discontent inside your team

Plan to weaken the negatives and strengthen the positives

It's no accident that we have grouped the positive and negative factors in the table above in such a way that shows some links from one side to the other. This is because our next step is to draw up a plan for each one, to strengthen or weaken it and there's often some common ground that you can use to affect both sides of the equation at the same time. In each case the aim is to focus on the issues that matter most to the people and the situation you're dealing with, tailoring the message so it strikes a chord.

Let's look at each pair of issues in turn.

Chief Executive and Line manager
In our list the CE's support is alongside a low level of
commitment from the immediate line manager. The link
here is that you could influence your line manager's level of
support by reinforcing to them that the CE is very much in
favour. You should do it subtly rather than in a
confrontational way. The plan here could be to:

- meet your line manager to give a progress
  report
- explain the benefits that come from the move
- make it clear that the CE sees those benefits
  and endorses them fully, and is looking for
  success
- remind your manager that you have talked it through
  in person with the CE, and that the support is still
  strong even though there was no more money
  available.

Being in the middle of a sandwich should focus the
manager's mind on the benefits. With you below and the
CE above, both aiming in the same direction, presenting
the case again may persuade the line manager that the
move has real benefits, if their lack of commitment is
based on logical argument. However, if – as is often the
case – their lack of enthusiasm stems more from fear of
taking a risk, getting involved in a difficult change and
possibly being associated with failure, then knowing that
the CE is behind the change should make a real
difference.

There's a spin-off, as well, that strengthens the positive side.
Having the line manager on board means that the CE sees a

united front, and will be reassured that their commitment is well placed.

Job security and resistance from the sitting tenants
It's always going to be difficult to win over the people you're displacing (including the staff's union representative).

You won't win them round by telling them how good it will be for you and your people – that's just adding insult to injury. They have to see some benefit for themselves, or they are simply losers in the shake-up.

The major benefit is the increased level of job security that comes from having the new premises. Their job is to support your section by doing the administration, so, if you succeed, they succeed as well.

Your plan could be to meet the union representative and explain the specifics of the market research, making it clear that the most important reason for the move is to protect jobs in both sections. This message strikes a chord because it adds a relevant and persuasive factor to the equation. You are selecting the information that matters to the union, who should be more concerned with big issues such as job security than with immediate moves from one place to another.

You could leave the message with the union representative and let it filter through to the staff. Or you might suggest they join you to present the key facts to the people in the other section, so you are winning the union representative round to your way of thinking. They won't convert from opposition to support overnight, but the balance of their thinking will have shifted in your favour.

Supporters and opponents inside the camp
Whenever you spot people who are going to oppose the change, it's natural to focus on them and spend a lot of time trying to win them round.

There is a real danger that you're just wasting your energy. Many people dislike change instinctively and you won't shift their position on that with all the logical arguments in the world. So you need to find another tactic.

You do have a positive side to this equation as most of your people are in favour, so the plan here should be to let the majority work on the minority for you. It's up to you whether you decide to share the benefits with everyone and let things take their course, or brief a couple of supporters to work on the opposition subtly and steadily. Either way, everyone is motivated to some degree by the need to be involved and be a respected member of a group, so the chances are that once those resisting see that everyone else is moving away from them, they will make at least some move to catch up and join them.

The bonus is that as the supporters try and win over the

opponents, they rehearse the arguments and benefits to the point where they take complete ownership of them. It's as if they invented the idea for themselves, as they champion the change on your behalf.

Plan for all the key factors

In these examples we've looked at some ways to strengthen the positive forces and undermine the negative ones. You have to go down the list and draw up a plan for each of your key factors – and your situation might mean that the examples we've used aren't the right ones for you. It all depends on your own situation and context.

Give everything a final check

Before you put your strategy into action, give it one last check-over. It's easy to lose sight of the main aims and get side-tracked as you draw up a strategy, so look at it all as a whole, to make sure it will help you achieve what you are aiming to achieve.

Summary

Today, we have looked at the need for a strategy – one that plans to deal with the forces that that are supporting your efforts, and to undermine those that are in opposition. If you follow this basic outline you won't go far wrong, but you will have noticed that most of the factors are about people and their attitudes.

To help you develop an even clearer insight into the reasons that people react as they do to change, we're going to look at some important points in more detail tomorrow.

If it weren't for the people ...

We saw earlier in the week that the real force for or against change is people and their emotions. That's why the most important factors in your strategic lists yesterday concern people and their reactions.

By using what you know about motivation you can work on tactics to win people round. Your aim is to increase the motivation for change and diminish the opposition. The key tactic is to think it through from their point of view – put yourself in their shoes and think about why they feel as they do. If you do that, you can find the right buttons to press. If you don't, you'll never win them round and you'll probably make things worse.

There are dozens of possible reasons for people resisting change, but two in particular play a powerful role in the process. We're going to work on these two, which are:

1 the fear of personal loss, while someone else wins
2 the feeling of being excluded, as if something is being done *to* them, rather than with their involvement.

Turning losers into winners

Some people resist change because they have logical and reasoned arguments against what is proposed. But it's far more likely that the real resistance – passive or active – comes when people assume that others will come out of it as winners, at their expense. Their immediate reaction is to look for the problems and the areas where they could lose out.

As a manager, you see the change from a different perspective and a different level. The list of benefits and drawbacks is about the organisation and/or your part of it, its processes, efficiency and effectiveness. You will spot things that they could lose, personally, but your management role helps provide a more balanced view.

These different perspectives are at the heart of the matter, because while you see the positives in the change, other people focus much more on what is negative for them.

Do you recall Pat's story, on Monday, where there were management job losses in the offing? These cuts obviously were good for the organisation, but they had a completely different meaning for Pat and Pat's colleagues. For them it was a personal survival issue. They changed the way they worked because their motivation patterns had altered fundamentally, in the face of a threat to their own well-being.

Your aim is to level out the effects so the losers don't lose out any more than they really have to. Start by working out what they might lose – or what they think they might – so that you can work to reassure them and raise their motivation levels.

What is at risk
During a potential change at work there are several areas where people fear they will lose something that matters to them. Four key ones are:

1 *Sense of direction*
   Change can upset a person's mental compass. At the moment they have a sense of direction and progress –

knowing where they started from and where they are heading. But they are frightened that they won't know where they are going when everything changes. They feel secure now so they are motivated, but the threat of losing a sense of security hits motivation hard. They can't see into the future so they don't know what the world will be like and how they can make sense of it all. Faced with all this, the natural reaction is to try and hang on to the present, so they resist the change in an attempt to prevent future uncertainty.

2 *Ability and competence*
People work hard to get the skills and knowledge needed to be good at their job. When a change is proposed they fear that those existing skills will not be enough, and that new skills and knowledge are needed for the new situation. It raises the spectre of failure ... and as fear of failure is an extremely powerful force it is not surprising that people dig their heels in and try and hang on to what they know.

3 *Seniority and status*

This links into the previous point. In the new order, will they have the same status they hold now – will they even have a job? For instance, take a situation where computers are coming to a department for the first time. A worker that everyone respects and looks up to, because of their experience and length of service, has never used one. They feel their ability is now in question, but they also face a potential drop down the pecking order. Recent school-leavers know much more about computers than they do, so there's a real fear that they'll lose the respect and seniority they are proud of.

4 *Friendships and networks*

Going to work in the same place, to do the same thing with the same people allows us to develop relationships with our colleagues. It helps build up a network of contacts to call on when we need help, a problem solved, or a favour. Moving offices, shifting to a new department or reorganising roles within a working group can affect friendships, and this is very unsettling. Even a small change – such as not sitting opposite the same person any more – threatens the stability of our relationships and causes resistance.

Take their fears seriously

This is a six-point checklist of common responses to other people's fears, which must be avoided. Never try and:

1 dismiss someone's fear as trivial, unreal or unfounded – if they perceive it as real, it's real for them (and that's what matters)
2 convince yourself that they haven't heard what's going on; they may not have heard the truth, but the grapevine

will have told them a good deal – some of it true and some of it complete exaggeration

3   change their views by telling them not to be so silly – that will just make them angry as well as worried

4   change their views with a logical explanation of the benefits for the organisation – they've dropped down the motivation ladder and they're concerned about themselves and their security

5   get them to see things from your point of view without taking their fears seriously – they will naturally see it from where they stand

6   convince them that you believe everything is positive and there are no problems – it makes a real difference if you share some of your own doubts and fears.

Motivation plays a major part in all these areas. People lose motivation when they're frightened, and you will only drive it further down if you rub salt in the wound and ignore their emotions, or try and bluster your way through.

On the other hand, to raise their commitment to you and the team, give them respect as team members, listen to them, take their fears seriously and communicate with them honestly and openly.

Winning them round
Of course, there are those issues that have to be kept under wraps – the sort of business issues we touched on yesterday. If there's a merger coming only the top people know about it, and there's virtually nothing anyone else can do to make it work, or to block it.

But most change isn't at that level; it's within the organisation and its departments. Success in this kind of everyday change depends on getting people to help make it work, under a good leader, because it is virtually impossible for any manager to implement a change successfully, in the face of total opposition from the team.

Lead from the middle
Leading from the middle – talking to people and sharing their fears and anxiety – is the only way to go.

This isn't just a moral issue; it's a pragmatic approach. If you think about the practical difference between being honest and trying to bluff your way through or keep it all secret, you'll see that bluffing and secrecy do no good at all. They will mistrust you from the start – and they already have the grapevine version, so your tight-lipped behaviour will exclude them and actually encourage rumours to flourish and grow.

Being as open as you can does not alter the reality of the situation. You can lose nothing, but you gain a lot by supporting the common motivational need to feel a sense of belonging, inclusion and personal worth. It also shows your people that you care about their situation, and that supports their need for security. And it avoids one of those key blocks to motivation, where they feel they are working for a manager who does not treat them properly and fairly.

Involvement and communication

The other key factor that causes people to resist change is the feeling that it is being done to them, without their having been asked, having any say in whether it's a good idea, or planning what will happen.

Among change management gurus, it has become an accepted truth that people do not really mind change, because they're used to it and they live with it every day of their lives. What they do mind is being changed.

The 'not invented here' syndrome

It's a strange fact of life that if front-line workers had been making the decisions, they might have invented exactly the same changes that someone else is now making them go through. The only difference when someone else imposes it on them is that they didn't decide it ... so they know it won't work ... and they're going to make sure that it doesn't.

To overcome this – and to increase your team's involvement and commitment to the change – you have to communicate like never before. They have to feel that they played a part in setting up the change – or at least had the chance to contribute to the detail – or it will be a 'not invented here' situation. And the bottom line is that you need the support and commitment of those who it's going to affect.

Some guidelines for communication

When you know a change is coming:

- communicate early (once you know that it is more than rumour) – it avoids the grapevine making things worse, and it makes the change more of a slope and less of a cliff face, when they reach it
- involve everyone whenever possible – talk to everyone individually, as a team, and in their working groups
- invite them to ask questions and ask for their help and ideas – the basic decision may be taken, but there's probably still a lot to decide in terms of the detail and the fine tuning
- share your own feelings – it's human to have some doubts and fears and it gets them on your side if they see that you are human too
- own the process, if it's a change you have to implement but did not decide – if you blame head office and say you hate it but it is going to happen, they will take their cue from you and resist with a vengeance
- keep the door open and keep the information flow going – by sending more information out you will nip any rumours in the bud, and you will also get more information back, about how things are within your team.

Choosing the right means of communication

Whenever possible, communicate face to face, either one to

one or within a team. Written communication is detached and distant, and the people it reaches can't ask questions or make a comment.

The medium and the message
When you receive news of something that directly affects you at work, how does it (or would it) feel if you received

the news through a terse message in management-speak, via an impersonal or general memo, circular or e-mail that went out to a fairly large group of people? The chances are that you'd feel uncomfortable, uncertain, or even shocked. It certainly wouldn't endear you to the sender, or to the change they had outlined.

Mass media, like memos and e-mail, deliver news quickly to a wide audience, but they are not right for sending personal messages about people's roles and their lives, or for broadcasting news of imminent change, or the planned effects that the change should have. They can be tempting because they're comfortable – nobody can answer back at the time, so you don't have to take any flak. But you inevitably store up more and much greater problems, because it's an impersonal and one-sided approach that doesn't allow for comments or questions.

The questions to ask are:

What effect will the way I communicate have on my colleagues' motivation and involvement?

How does the means of communication and the language I use affect the emotions and the likely behaviour of the people receiving it?

A case in point
The MD sends out a newsletter, saying that changes are on the way to steer the company in a new, hopefully more profitable, direction, and that most departments will have to adapt their roles and practices. The MD is concerned about profit and the interests of shareholders. Despite the fact that the changes will affect virtually everyone, it's too expensive and too much of a chore to tell them individually, or try and help them come to terms with it.

When the unions threaten industrial action and individuals stop performing as they have been doing, the MD blames them for being reactionary and 'failing to grasp the opportunity to stride together into a more profitable and secure future'.

But it's the MD who got it wrong, by losing sight of the fact that organisations are made up of people, and people have emotions. For the workforce it isn't a logical issue about business efficiency, it's an emotional issue about their own futures and their sense of security.

Telling is not selling
Working to gain commitment is like trying to get an order

for a new product. It means selling the idea that this change is worthwhile, and that the benefits – for them – outweigh the disadvantages. In change management, like in sales, the one approach that is guaranteed to fail is to assume that if you say it loudly enough and often enough, people believe it.

Involve and communicate

To put it simply, the less you involve people with the change that's taking place, the less opportunity you give them to help you and the more they feel that it's being done to them, rather than with them or for them.

Facing up to reality
Facing people and sharing information and feelings with them is a scary prospect, because of the assumption that they're going to be awkward. Unfortunately, they probably will be – at the start. It's a fact of the process, but it has to be faced. Many managers don't face it though, and put off the evil day by telling themselves they'll wait until there's more to say or they have a clearer picture. These excuses are quite understandable, but they are not acceptable and they are certainly not going to help in the long run.

Involving people at the earliest possible stage limits the amount of rumour and suspicion you have to confront. It offers a better prospect of creating a dialogue that can build trust, openness and mutual respect. Shutting them out just reduces the potential for them to get excited and motivated about the change, because they have no stake in the outcomes or the process.

Bringing it down to a personal level
Think about the most effective way to get an individual to

change their behaviour – maybe someone working for you who is very abrupt with their colleagues, who feel it's close to aggressiveness. You need to do something, or it could quickly end up as a grievance or a disciplinary issue.

It's not easy to grasp the nettle and open it up with them, but it must be done. Leave it and it can only fester and develop into a full-blown problem.

You could read them the riot act and tell them to pull their socks up or else. You could ... but you'd be wasting everyone's time. The individual concerned might put on a smile while you're around, but they'd resent it and take it out on their colleagues, or play some sort of game to get even.

The best way to bring about a behaviour change is to follow these eight steps.

1 Sit them down and start by praising them for something they do well – that way they're ready to hear more.
2 Explain carefully and sensitively that you have observed some problems, describing actual behaviour and its effects (when you did x ... the result I saw was ...) and avoiding generalisations or value judgements (it's not good enough ... people don't like it).
3 Find out – and help them find out – why they behave the way they do, by asking open questions (what, why, how etc).
4 Explain the benefits of changing their behaviour – for them (better relationships, higher popularity, less stress etc), their colleagues (a higher regard for the individual, better team feeling, less stress etc), and for you (less upset, more output, better working relationships and atmosphere etc).

5 Get their acceptance that they can change – they are capable of it.

6 Discuss how to make a change, ensuring they don't lose by experiencing a loss of face, or public humiliation.

7 Agree a plan for change and set some targets, starting with some easy first steps to build confidence – nothing succeeds like success.

8 Watch progress and give feedback on how things are going, to reinforce success and discourage them from slipping back.

Scale it up

This model is about involvement, sharing information and working together to achieve change. The example is about an individual changing, but the principles apply just as much to groups, and to more major changes. So scale it up and use the above eight-point plan to develop the right sort of involvement for yourself.

Real communication

Communication is not just about passing on information. Real communication is always two way – especially in times of change. This means sharing what you know and feel in one direction, and inviting comments, ideas, concerns and difficulties in the other direction.

There are at least three good reasons for this.

1 It reduces the ever-present chance of rumour overtaking fact. People who are misinformed or not told enough will interpret what they've heard and fill in the gaps themselves, resulting in panic, paranoia and general bad feeling.

2 It makes for stronger and more loyal relationships,

because people really do appreciate being spoken to and listened to. This is always important and beneficial, but especially so during uncertain and potentially unstable circumstances.

3 It links straight back into what you know about motivation. Poor management and supervision is a major block, while responsibility and a share in decision-making is a positive motivating factor.

Summary

Resistance to change is based much more on fear of loss and fear of the unknown, than it is on logical argument. Success comes from working to understand people's fears, and helping them feel less threatened.

The solutions lie in motivation – knowing what affects your people, so you can start helping them feel more confident about an uncertain future. Poor communication and actions that exclude people are bound to lead to problems, so the key messages are to communicate like never before, and involve people in their own futures, as early as possible.

Tomorrow, we are looking at how to work with individuals, so as to help them give the sort of commitment you need, to make the change happen successfully.

Working on commitment

We saw yesterday that most people are threatened by change. They're either going to lose something or they fear they will. We need to work on their attitudes and beliefs – from their perspective not ours.

Today, we look at how to handle different people – either leaving them alone, harnessing their enthusiasm, or planning ways to influence their level of commitment where they influence your chances of success.

We all see it differently

Not everyone views the prospect of change in the same way. Like everything in life, there is a tiny minority at either extreme of the situation. At one end, there are a few who will resist any change, on principle. Nothing you can do or say will move these 'negs' from their 100% negative stance.

At the other extreme, there is an equally small group who are actually turned on by the prospect of change – either any change, or more productively, this particular change. These 'change fans' only seem to be buzzing when something major is in a state of flux.

Handling the extremists
When confronted by a complete 'neg', the immediate temptation is to put all your efforts into trying to win them round. You concentrate on arguing, cajoling and trying to get them to see sense. It turns into a personal challenge – almost a mission.

Don't bother.

You can't win, and all that happens is that you spend 90% of your time and energy on 10% of the problem – and it's the insoluble 10% at that!

Instead, accept reality and take a detour, right round them. Get the other 90% working with you and you can make it – so concentrate on the change fans and the majority in the middle. Once the change has happened and the dust has settled, the 'negs' will come round, quietly move across and rejoin the mainstream, because it's human nature not to stay isolated.

Use the change fans differently. If you find people who are really fired up by the prospect of the change, make them your change champions and send them out as missionaries. If they are briefed properly, their enthusiasm and commitment when they talk to other groups and individuals will make a real difference to the unsure and unsettled majority.

The majority

Most people lie between these extremes – somewhere in the middle. They have fears and anxieties, but you can win them round if you work at it, using the right approach.

Winning the majority round means involving and communicating with groups and teams, on the lines we looked at yesterday. It would be great if you could talk to everyone individually, but the reality is that there simply isn't the time – although your change champions can help share the load.

However, there are always some key individuals that you do need to concentrate on.

Looking at individuals

We know from analysing the forces for and against change on Wednesday, that people are the most powerful force of all. There are some who could be very helpful and others who are potential problems.

The job of implementing the change would be so much more straightforward if we could alter these individual's levels of commitment. And there is a way – but it means taking a strategic view of precisely where those people sit, relative to your aims.

The stages in a commitment strategy

The technique for planning and working on people's commitment (positive and negative) during change, follows these three steps.

1 Identify all the key people and 'map' where you feel each one is now.
2 Then work out where you need them to be, on that same continuum.
3 Now you know where they are and where you want them to be, work out a plan to shift their commitment nearer to your ideal.

Steps 1 and 2 require a basic grid. We'll look at how it works, using a simple case study. We'll look at an example from the NHS, but you could easily substitute something commercial from your own experience.

NHS case study

A survey shows that out-patients in a small NHS clinic would like to see some changes. One of their main complaints is that they wait a long time to be seen, and are then sent all round the hospital. Someone who knows they'll need an X-ray this time still has to wait for ages to see the doctor first.

It takes the doctor ten seconds to say they can't be examined without an X-ray. So the patient leaves the consulting room and heads for radiography, where they join the back of the queue, have the X-ray and then wait for the films to be developed. Then it's back to the clinic ... where they join the back of the queue again.

The change being planned is simple – whatever is decided at the end of the previous appointment is carried out at the start of the next one. So someone needing an X-ray skips the initial wait for the consultant, and is sent first to radiography. They bring the X-ray back with them and are then seen.

The people involved in the change are the consultant, the radiographer, the receptionist, a nurse and a nurse manager. The consultant's opinion is crucial, but because it doesn't affect her own workload, her support at the moment is barely lukewarm. The nurse is keen because he believes patients will get a better deal. So is the nurse manager, although she is worried about losing control, and concerned that it might be more work. The receptionist is extremely enthusiastic – it would stop everyone moaning to him about having to wait – but his enthusiasm gets on the nurse manager's nerves. The radiographer dislikes change and wants things to stay as they are.

Step 1: Identifying and mapping the key people
Draw up a grid and list the people you are concerned about, in the left-hand column. Then mark their level of commitment with a 'C' (for 'Current') at the appropriate point on the scale. You may have to estimate this, for certain people, but the chances are that you can do this fairly accurately.

The highest level of commitment is 'Driving', where the individual works actively to make the change happen. Then comes 'Supporting', less up-front but still positive. 'Accepting' is a fairly passive approach, not blocking but not pushing for change either. 'Resisting' speaks for itself.

This is how the grid looks so far, for our NHS example.

Key people	Resisting	Accepting	Supporting	Driving
Consultant		C		
Receptionist				C
Nurse			C	
Nurse manager		C		
Radiographer	C			

Step 2: Work out where you want them to be
Now mark an 'F' ('Future') where you want them to be. Keep it realistic; for instance, the radiographer is never going to be a change champion, so place him slightly nearer the right, but not at an unreasonable spot.

Some people have the C and the F together, if their current level of commitment is OK. Others have the F to the right of the C and a few may have it to the left, where you need someone to calm down a bit because their enthusiasm is putting others off (as the receptionist is).

Putting in an arrow shows the direction and the distance you want individuals to shift. The NHS example now looks like this.

Key people	Resisting	Accepting	Supporting	Driving
Consultant		C ──────────────▶		F
Receptionist			F ◀────────	C
Nurse			CF	
Nurse manager		C ──────▶ F		
Radiographer	C ──────▶ F			

Step 3: Plan to shift them

Now you know where each key person is and how far you would like them to shift, you work out individual plans to help make them move.

Pay most attention to the really key people – the ones who exercise the greatest influence. Make these your prime targets ... but work on everyone.

Using what you know about motivation, work out or find out why they feel as they do, and what would affect their commitment. This provides the agenda for talking to them individually – and it's their agenda, not yours.

For instance, the consultant might be keen to improve the system for patients, but doesn't understand the depth of feeling. In that case, some direct feedback from patients might tip the balance. Or she may like to develop a reputation as an innovator by helping to lead the change. Perhaps, if she knew that patients feel she is in charge of the system and blame her personally, she may want to look better in their eyes.

The bottom line is that it doesn't affect her workload

anyway, so she has nothing to lose. This means it is just a question of identifying how she can win.

The receptionist could well respond to an open chat about the effect their enthusiasm is having. He wants the change, so once he understands the situation he would probably adapt his behaviour as a positive contribution.

For each individual there is a formula, somewhere, for pressing the right motivational buttons and creating movement in the direction you want.

Summary

It's wrong to make assumptions about how people view change – both in general and any specific change they're facing.

Some people are totally opposed and others are very keen. Once you know who fits where you can manage them and their responses constructively – either ignoring them or using them as champions.

Working with the majority of people – those who aren't at the extremes – you can analyse and alter their level of commitment.

We've looked today at some techniques for working out who fits where, and how to handle them. They are not complicated, and using them increases your chances of success and makes the process less stressful all round.

We're nearly at the end of the week, so now that we have looked at the underlying issues and techniques, it's time tomorrow to put a plan together and start to make the change happen.

Making the change happen

Now that you have explored the steps towards winning people round to change, it's time to put it all into practice.

A team: greater than the sum of the parts

You could try and lead the change on your own, but the chances are that going it alone would make it too great a task.

Putting a team together adds value to the process, for you and the team members. For you, a team:

- allows you to allocate tasks around several people, instead of having to tackle them all yourself
- lets you bring together a range of expertise and experience, to cover all the details and technical issues that figure in the change
- brings any change champions into the heart of the process, keeping them fully informed and using their commitment to the full
- means you have direct involvement and communication, even if it is only with a small group of people
- brings other brains to the process, so that your combined creativity is applied
- avoids any one individual being seen as the only person driving things forward.

For team members it satisfies several of their most powerful motivational needs, as they:

- take on a higher level of responsibility and recognition
- take part in the decision-making that affects their lives
- have a worthwhile job to do
- see the results of their efforts.

Picking the team

Try to keep the size of the team manageable – four or five people works well. There's no point in selecting people who are unshakeably opposed to the change you're working on. But it is worth thinking about those individuals who are not 100% sure. Bringing someone into the management process can be a way of raising their level of commitment, as it gives them a stake in the team's operations, once they are part of the process.

Generally, the team is made up of people who have one of two characteristics – and ideally, both:

1 They are at least supportive, on the commitment grid.
2 They have some particular skills that are needed to
   achieve success – either in a technical or other specialist
   areas or in 'people skills' so they can help work on the
   human side of the equation.

Your first task
Your first task is to help the selected individuals start to
work as an effective team. Unlike other groups, teams have
special characteristics and needs that have to be clarified
and developed. For instance:

- a team has to have a clear and common
  understanding of its aims and objectives
- the team members' various roles need to be
  explored and clarified
- a team has to have a higher level of openness, trust
  and mutual support than there is in ordinary work
  groups
- a team has its own operating procedures and
  working practices.

As the leader, you help set the vision, clarify the objectives
and sort out the roles and operating procedure, in exactly
the same way as you would for any other team. You can
find detailed help in one of the many guides to building
teams, including *Successful Teambuilding in a week*.

Building the plan

The team needs a plan to work to. The plan itself is an
essential tool, and the process of building the plan helps
form and bond the team.

Create the vision

Having a broad destination in mind helps keep the process on course, so before getting into detail, develop a 'crystal ball' vision of the future by thinking about what the world will look like once the change is in place.

Always remember that your aim is not to stick to the plan at all costs: it is to reach your destination by whatever means are best. Your detailed plan is a useful map or chart, guiding you towards the final destination. But it is a means to an end, and not a set of rules to follow slavishly.

So if you find that you have been blown off course at any stage in the process, as long as you have a vision of your overall destination, you can find alternative routes or detours that will still get you home.

Set some milestones

Once the vision is clear, set some milestones at the critical points. For instance, if the change is an office move, you could decide that:

- milestone 1 is reached when you have talked to everyone involved
- milestone 2 is when you have drawn up the schedule of new furniture and equipment needed, and old stuff that has to be disposed of
- milestone 3 is the floor plan of the new office – who sits where
- the final milestone is the move itself, when everyone is in place.

Milestones help break the whole process down into manageable objectives.

Set the objectives
The plan itself really starts with a clear set of objectives. Stating what has to be achieved sets out the framework for the action. It also provides the means of knowing when you've arrived. Objectives have to be very clear and precise, and should follow the SMART principles. This means they are:

- **S**pecific: leaving no doubt or room for confusion or interpretation
- **M**easurable: how many and/or how much
- **A**chievable: not an impractical wish list, but possible (if challenging)
- **R**ealistic: with the resources available, in the context you work in
- **T**ime-scaled: by when.

Getting the details clear

Some plans look incredibly complex and technical, especially if they use some of the common project-planning techniques like critical path analysis, networks and Gantt charts, whether on paper or computer software.

But any plan is a simple set of details, that makes sense to everyone who is using it and provides an at-a-glance way of checking how things are going.

Break it down

There are only four components to a plan. The first three are:

1   what has to be done
2   who does it
3   by when.

The fourth component is to find any dependencies, which simply means, work out what has to happen before we can do this. Spotting the dependencies is where the more complicated project-planning techniques come into their own. But it isn't that hard to do, if you start at the end and work backwards.

A backwards look at a plan
Starting at the end:

- decide when the change has to be completed by, as an end date
- use the vision and the objectives to spell out your definition of success; remember, this is the final milestone
- identify what has to be done to reach this final milestone (you'll find you can't do activity X until Y is complete, or until Y and Z both are)
- carry the pattern on, as Y and Z depend in turn on, say, A, B and C
- set timescales for each activity.

When you reach the beginning you'll probably have some activities that simply don't fit the timescales, that you've squeezed in to make it look as if it works. In that case go back over it all and re-assess the dependencies and the timings. You must have a workable plan – not a wish list.

If you can't make it all work out in the time, there are only three options:

1 ignore the fact and start work, hoping that a small miracle will occur about the middle of the process
2 change the plan again, and either tighten up the timings or scale down the objectives
3 move the end date to something that is realistic.

The first option is not really an option. It is a very common approach, but it leads directly to frustration and failure, so do not even think about it!!

The heart of the plan
This is really straightforward, as long as you have taken the other preliminary steps, because the heart of the plan is a list or table like this.

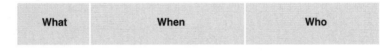

What	When	Who

It really is this simple.

> • In the left column the team specifies what is to be done, using the SMART approach so there's no room for ambiguity or assumptions.
> • The centre column says when it is to be done by – realistically.
> • The column on the right spells out who does it, either one name or a group, with one person identified as the coordinator.

The result is a clear and complete breakdown of the actions and steps needed to bring the plan to fruition.

Three points to bear in mind

1 As long as you have put it together with care, trust the plan. If there is a slight wobble in the middle of the process, don't panic and throw the whole thing away and start again.
2 However, the plan is a servant, not the master; the

details can always be changed to reach the overall destination, by adjusting the timings or finding a different route between two specific points.

3 The plan not only sets the route out in advance, it provides a map that you should use to monitor progress; if you're not where you thought you would be, on time, you have an early warning that you need to get the team together to look at some other action, outside the plan.

The importance of monitoring progress

The third point in this list – monitoring progress – is especially important. As the plan unfolds, have regular team meetings to keep an eye on how it's going, with everyone sharing views and ideas for fine tuning. In this way you will stay on course for your destination.

You also maintain motivation, by having regular team meetings. As we saw on Monday, the lack of effective management is a serious motivational blockage, so leading the team from the middle ensures that this doesn't apply. There are a couple of specific actions you should take during team meetings, to maintain motivation and keep commitment high.

1 Praise the team and its members for what they get right and give them constructive feedback about things that could have been better; knowing how you're doing is a positive motivator.

2 Let the team find solutions to problem; don't close them down and impose your will, because it undermines their commitment and morale.

You have arrived

In a few weeks, what was new will feel well established and normal, as if it has always been this way. In fact, try and change it now and you're back at the top of the process.

You know you've reached your destination because the vision has become a reality, and you can tick off all the objectives, one by one.

When the process is over and the change is in place, have a team party to celebrate success. Saying thank you and taking pleasure in a job well done are both far too uncommon ... and they really do help keep morale high.

At that final meeting, review the whole process and identify any real successes and any areas that could have been done better. They both provide useful pointers for the next time you have to plan a change.

Summary

There is no substitute for a sound plan. It helps you see the way ahead, and stay on course when things get tough.

Neither is there a real substitute for using a team to help plan and implement the change, unless it is on such a small scale that it doesn't need more than one person.

By weaving the threads of motivation into the change process, you can achieve the outcomes you want and not only avoid change being a negative process, but turn it round and make it a positive and constructive way of developing sound working relationships.

Conclusion

Throughout the week we have linked change to motivation, because change is essentially about people, their emotional reactions and their commitment. We have looked at the unique way that individuals see the world, and discovered that patterns of motivation change as circumstances change.

This link between motivation and change is often overlooked, but working on the motivation and commitment of individuals during a time of change is even more crucial than at other times.

Change is inherently threatening, bringing the fear of loss. But not everyone sees change in the same way, so it's important to find out who you can work with and who is critical to your success. Then you can use a range of techniques to quantify the change and analyse how to affect commitment levels among the people who can help or block progress.

Now you are ready to make the change happen, developing a team to plan and implement the key activities that will get you to your destination. The plan is a vital tool, but it is not a tablet of stone. Flexibility is a key factor.

Remember that it could always be done better, so learn the lessons from each change management experience and apply them the next time there's a need to make a change.

Further *Successful Business in a Week* **titles from** Hodder & Stoughton and the Institute of Management all at £6.99

All Hodder & Stoughton books are available from your local bookshop or can be ordered direct from the publisher. Just tick the titles you want and fill in the form below. Prices and availability subject to change without notice.

To: Hodder & Stoughton Ltd, Cash Sales Department, Bookpoint, 39 Milton Park, Abingdon, Oxon, OX14 4TD. If you have a credit card you may order by telephone – 01235 400414.

E-mail address: orders@bookpoint.co.uk

Please enclose a cheque or postal order made payable to Bookpoint Ltd to the value of the cover price and allow the following for postage and packaging:

UK & BFPO: £4.30 for one book; £6.30 for two books; £8.30 for three books.

OVERSEAS & EIRE: £4.80 for one book; £7.10 for 2 or 3 books (surface mail).

Name: ....

Address: ....

....

If you would prefer to pay by credit card, please complete:

Please debit my Visa/Mastercard/Diner's Card/American Express (delete as appropriate) card no:

❑❑❑❑❑❑❑❑❑❑❑❑❑❑❑❑❑❑

Signature .... Expiry Date ....